THE CONTROLLERS

A VIEW OF OUR RESPONSIBILITY

By
JIM
COLE

Illustrated
by
Tom
Woodruff

Published by   **G** **GROWING**
IMAGES

Distributed   by

Ed and Janet Reynolds
37 Lomita Drive
Mill Valley, California
94941

ISBN 0-9601200-2-5 $4.95

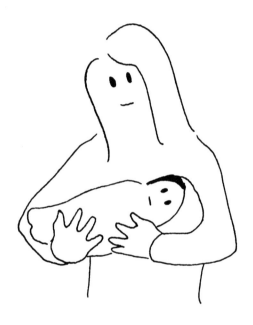

At first I was held and
completely cared for
by others.

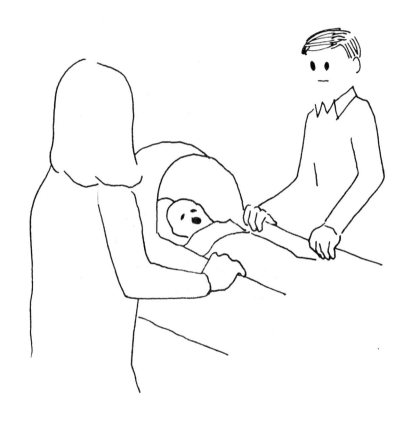

I was helpless and could do nothing for myself so they decided everything for me.

When I did something, someone
else took the responsibility

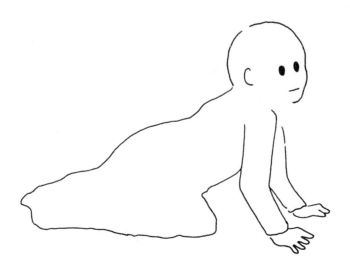

because they had control
over me.

Slowly their control became less complete

and less direct.

People expected me to do things
that I didn't want to do,

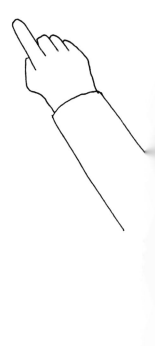

and I was afraid to say,
"I don't want to."

So I developed controllers,

and I gave the controller
the responsibility.

No one can see my controllers,

so I tell people about them.

Often I tell people about my
controllers in little ways.

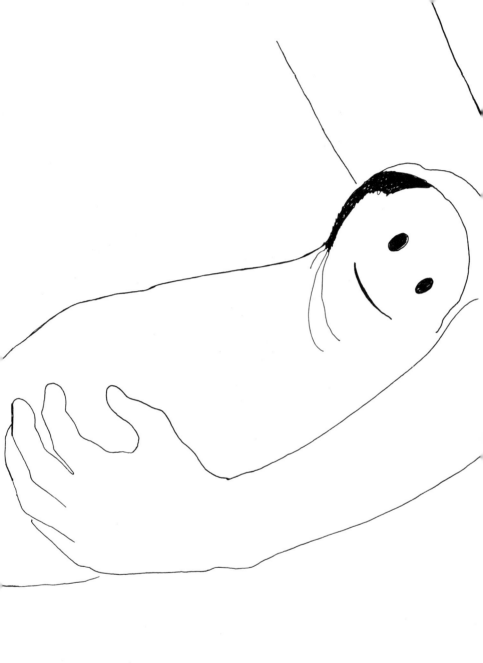

While my Parents were warm,
close, and certain in their
control,

the new controllers are not.

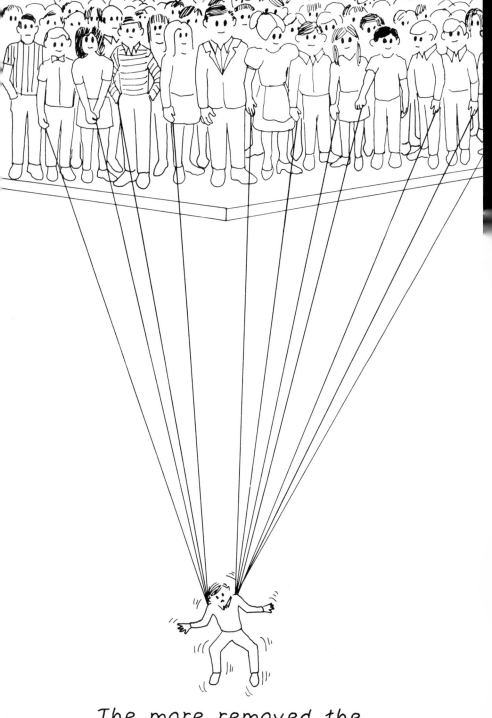

The more removed the
controllers are from me, the
more of them I need,

and the more uncertain I feel.

To overcome my uncertainty, I spend much of my time looking for new controllers.

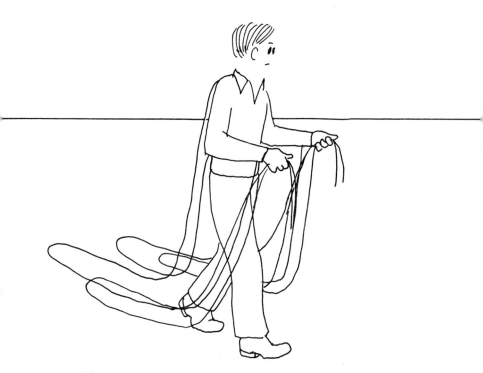

I have many ways of getting new controllers.

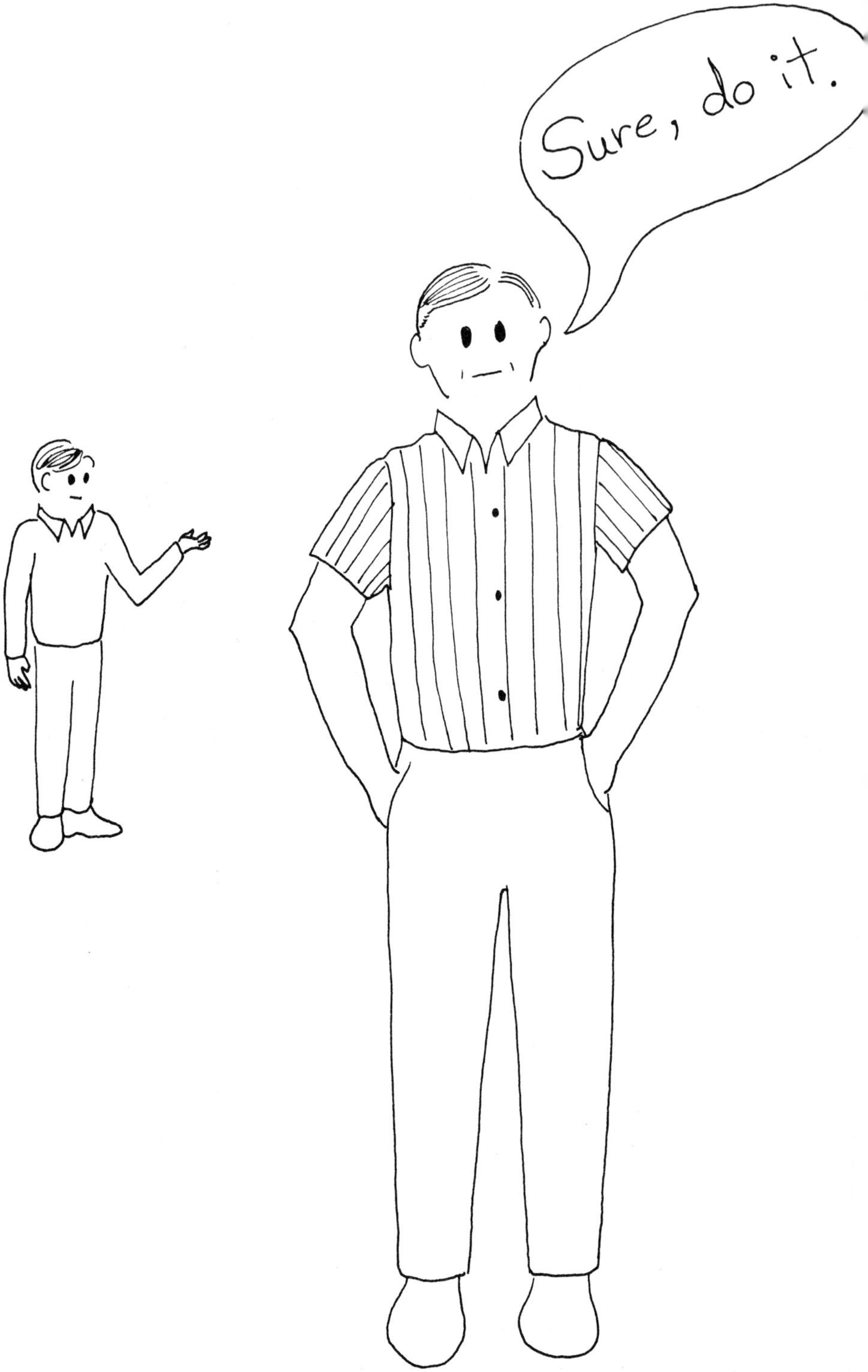
Sure, do it.

Sometimes after I have already done something, I look for a controller.

My controller
doesn't need to
know that I've
made him my
controller.

But I often let
him know that I
have made him
responsible for
my feelings.

Sometimes I try to give
someone my controls,

and he won't take them,

and I feel helpless.

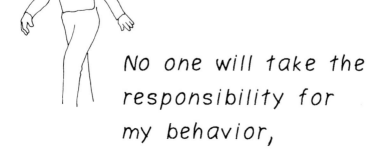

so I build controllers of what
I'm afraid they will want.

The controllers I make of fears
don't comfort me,

so I comfort myself with controllers from my past.

Sometimes I become frightened and yell for help.

Someone tries to help me become
free from my controllers,

and I make him a controller.

I spend a lot of time
telling myself and others
I'm controlled.

While I'm complaining abou
my controllers,

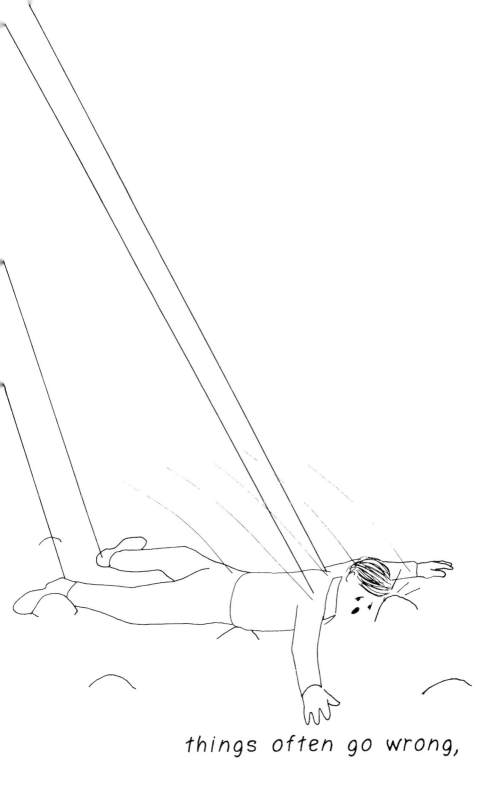

things often go wrong,

and it's all
their fault.

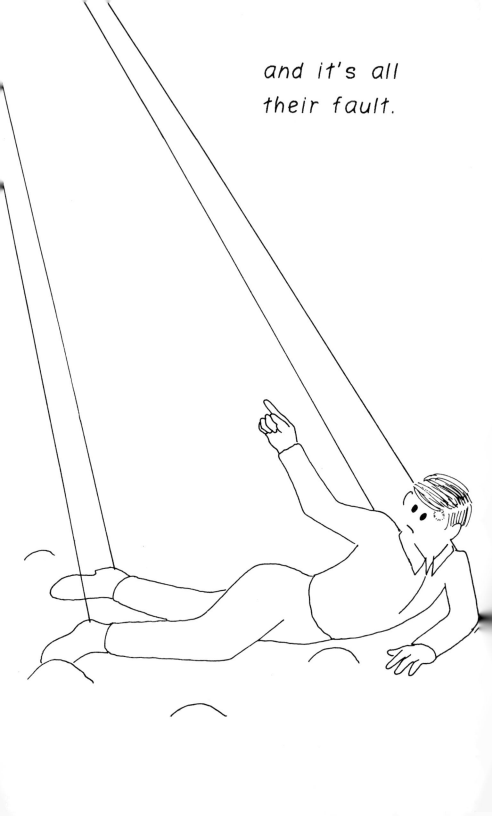

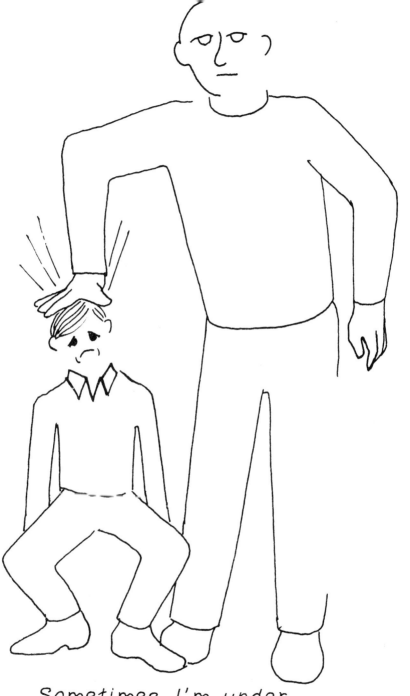

Sometimes I'm under
real pressure,

but the pressure does not
have control of me.

nly if I make
t my controller does the
ressure have control of me.

Then I work to keep the
pressure in control.

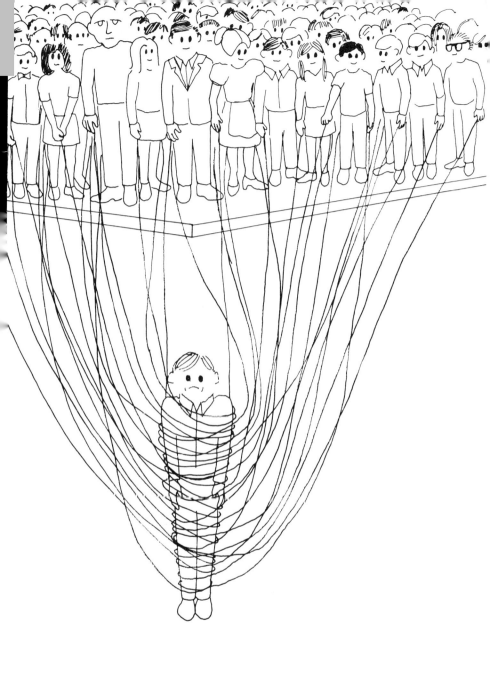

I often feel very restricted
by the controllers.

I forget that I created the controllers, and I decide who will be responsible.

Sometimes I know I am responsible
for what I have done.

Then I see my controllers,

and the controllers
get the credit.

So I become a controller
to get the credit.

When the other person
falls, I get hurt,

and I
get blamed.

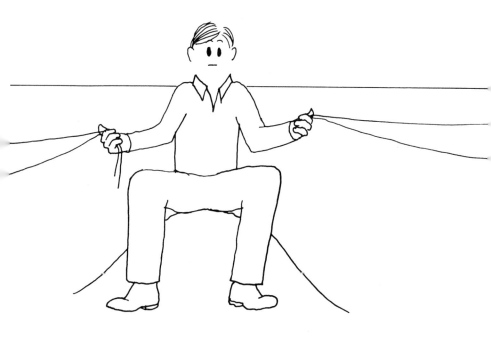

I cannot control others
and be free myself.

Sometimes I work very hard
to prove that I am free,

but I am not free and I know it.

Sometimes I think I am free and I want others to stop using controllers.

Then I discover that I am trying
to become a controller myself.

As I learn to live without controllers, I feel less of need to control others.

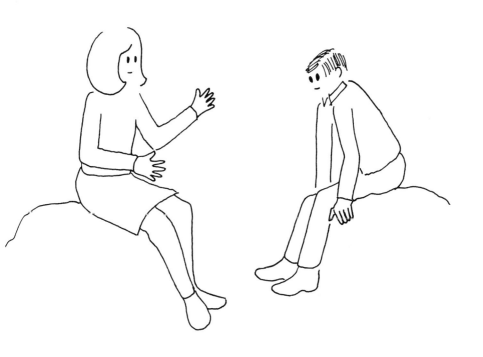

There are times when someone
near me isn't using controllers.

This makes it harder for me
to use my controllers and I
am frightened,

so I try to create controllers for the other person.

After collecting controllers
for a long time, I have more
controllers than I can ever us

and my controllers disagree
on what I should do.

None of my controllers will
really be responsible for my
behavior.

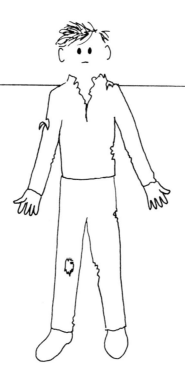

I alone am responsible for
my behavior.

There is no one to take the
responsibility for my behavior

There never really was.

The more I take the
responsibility for my
own behavior,

the more I want the
responsibility and the less
I use the controllers.

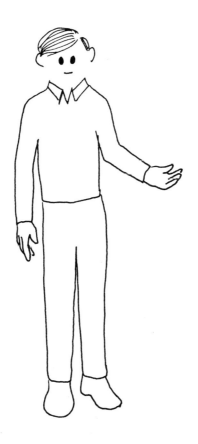

Sometimes I am free.

My being responsible may make
another person feel uncertain,

so the other person tries to
create controllers for me.

It doesn't work because I am
the only person

who can ever create
controllers for me.

The more I live without the
controllers,the more I grow
to understand

that I am free only
when I am responsible.

OTHER BOOKS BY JIM COLE

The Facade is a view of how we resist
sharing our personal selves with others.

$2.75

Filtering People explores the
growth, use, and function of
prejudices. It examines how
prejudices "protect us",
isolate us, and disrupt our
relationships with others.
It suggests some responses
to both our own feelings of
prejudice and those of other

$9.95